Darrin Lunde

Illustrated by Patricia J. Wynne

Hello, Mama Wallaroo

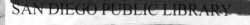

■ Charlesbridge

Hello, hopping animal.
What is your name?

My name is Mama Wallaroo.

A wallaroo is a kind of kangaroo.

Mama Wallaroo, what do you look like?

I have a long face and a long tail.

I have big ears and big feet.

Mama Wallaroo, how tall are you?

I am about three feet tall.

Mama Wallaroo, where do you live?

I live in Australia.

I like rocky hillsides.

Mama Wallaroo, what do you eat?

I graze on grass all day.

Mama Wallaroo, how do you move?

I use my big feet to hop from rock to rock.

Mama Wallaroo, what do you fear?

I am afraid of dingoes.

They try to eat me.

I hop away when I see them.

Mama Wallaroo, what is in your pouch?

My baby is in my pouch.

I hop with him inside.

Mama Wallaroo, when do you sleep?

I sleep in the shade in the
middle of the day.
I don't like bright sun.

Sleep well,
Mama Wallaroo!

A newborn wallaroo is smaller than a mouse.

Baby wallaroos are called joeys.

A joey drinks its mother's milk from inside the pouch.

A joey leaves its mother's pouch after six months.

It usually stays with its mother for another year and a half.

Male wallaroos sometimes fight for mates.
They kick each other with their big feet.

There are about fifty different kinds of
kangaroo-like animals in Australia.

For Asahi—D. L.

For my friend Patricia Brunauer,
with gratitude—P. J. W.

Published by Charlesbridge
85 Main Street
Watertown, MA 02472
(617) 926-0329
www.charlesbridge.com

Library of Congress Cataloging-in-Publication Data
Lunde, Darrin P.
    Hello, mama wallaroo / Darrin Lunde ; illustrated by Patricia J. Wynne.
        p. cm.
Audience: 3-6.
    ISBN 978-1-57091-796-7 (reinforced for library use)
    ISBN 978-1-57091-797-4 (softcover)
    ISBN 978-1-60734-605-0 (ebook)
1. Common wallaroo—Juvenile literature.
2. Kangaroos—Juvenile literature. I. Title.
QL737.M35L85 2013
599.2'2—dc23   2012024436

Printed in Singapore
(hc) 10 9 8 7 6 5 4 3 2 1
(sc) 10 9 8 7 6 5 4 3 2 1

Illustrations done in watercolor, ink, and colored pencil on Arches hot-press paper
Display type and text type set in Garamouche Bold from P22 Type Foundry and Billy from SparkyType
Color separations by KHL Chroma Graphics, Singapore
Printed and bound February 2013 by Imago in Singapore
Production supervision by Brian G. Walker
Designed by Martha MacLeod Sikkema